Change the Mind, Change the Man

A Scriptural Study Guide

For Use with Prison Ministries, Reentry Programs,
Congregational Studies, and Families

Paul Hainline

Contents

How to Use This Guide

Part One — The Descent: The Mind Turning Away

Week 1   The Phone Call

Week 2   The Progression

Week 3   Where Did We Go Wrong?

Week 4   All of the Imprisoned Aren't in Prison

Week 5   Love That Says No

Week 6   Think

Part Two — The Return: The Mind Turning Back

Week 7   Coming to Himself

Week 8   The Father Ran

Week 9   The Long Road

Week 10   The God Who Finds You

How to Use This Guide

This study guide is designed to accompany *Change the Mind, Change the Man* by Paul Hainline. It follows the book chapter by chapter, one week at a time, over ten weeks.

But the book is not the curriculum. The Bible is.

Each week, the group reads a chapter from the book. Then they go to the Scriptures that chapter opens up — and they stay there. The chapter is the door. The Scripture is the room. Every question in this guide sends the group into the biblical text, not back into the book. The book tells you where to look. The Bible tells you what to see.

The Two Tracks

The book speaks to two audiences simultaneously — the person struggling with addiction and the family carrying the weight. This study guide does the same. Each week includes two tracks of discussion questions:

Track A is for the one in the struggle. **Track B** is for the family.

If your group is all one audience — a prison ministry group, for example, or a family support group — use the track that fits. If your group includes both, use both. The two audiences are living inside the same story. They belong in the same room.

For the Group Leader

Your job is simple, and it is the same every week: keep the group in the text.

When someone shares an opinion, ask: "Where do you see that in the passage?" When someone drifts into generalities, bring them back: "Let's look at the verse again." When someone opens up honestly — let them. Don't rush to fix it. The text is already doing the work.

You are doing what a faithful Bible teacher does. You are asking, "Let's see what the Bible says." And then you are letting it say it.

THE DESCENT: THE MIND TURNING AWAY

THE PHONE CALL

Chapter 1 — "The Phone Call"

Before the Group Meets

Read Chapter 1 of *Change the Mind, Change the Man.*

Then read the following passages — slowly, more than once — before you come to the group:

- **Psalm 23:1-6** (the entire psalm — it's six verses; give it the time it deserves)
- **James 1:2-4**
- **Psalm 34:17-18**

Opening

Have someone read Psalm 23:4 aloud to the group.

> *"Even though I walk through the valley of the shadow of death, I fear no evil, for You are with me; Your rod and Your staff, they comfort me."*

Then ask: **What is the one word in this verse that changes everything?**

The word is *through.* Not "into." Not "around." Not "stuck in." The valley has a *through.* David does not describe a dead end. He describes a passage — dark, frightening, shadowed by death — but a passage nonetheless. You are not reading this book, and you are not sitting in this group, because everything is fine. Something brought you here. And the first thing Scripture says about the darkest valley is that it has an other side.

Into the Text

Passage 1 — Psalm 23:1-4

"The LORD is my shepherd, I shall not want. He makes me lie down in green pastures; He leads me beside quiet waters. He restores my soul; He guides me in the paths of righteousness for His name's sake. Even though I walk through the valley of the shadow of death, I fear no evil, for You are with me; Your rod and Your staff, they comfort me."

Questions:

1. Notice the shift in pronouns. In verses 1-3, David speaks *about* God: "He makes me lie down... He leads me... He restores my soul." But in verse 4, David begins speaking *to* God: "You are with me; Your rod and Your staff, they comfort me." Why does the conversation become personal when the valley appears? What does that tell you about where God is when the crisis hits?

2. Verse 3 says "He restores my soul." The Hebrew word for "restores" (*shub*) means to turn back, to return. It is the same word used throughout the Old Testament for repentance — for turning back to God. What does it mean that the Shepherd *restores* — turns back — the soul? Who is doing the work in that phrase?

3. The psalm does not say "I will never walk through the valley." It says "even though I walk through" it. The valley is not a sign that God has abandoned you. It is a place where God walks with you. For someone in crisis — whether the addict or the family — why does that distinction matter?

Passage 2 — James 1:2-4

"Consider it all joy, my brethren, when you encounter various trials, knowing that the testing of your faith produces endurance. And let endurance have its perfect result, so that you may be perfect and complete, lacking in nothing."

Questions:

4. James says "consider it all joy" — not "feel joy." The word "consider" is a deliberate, rational act. James is not asking you to feel happy about suffering. He is asking you to *think* about it in a specific way. What is the specific way? What does the testing produce?

5. Verse 4 says endurance must "have its perfect result." That means endurance is not the end — it is producing something. What is it producing? And what does "perfect and complete, lacking in nothing" look like for someone just beginning this journey?

Passage 3 — Psalm 34:17-18

"The righteous cry, and the LORD hears and delivers them out of all their troubles. The LORD is near to the brokenhearted and saves those who are crushed in spirit."

Questions:

6. Who does the Lord draw near to, according to verse 18? Not the strong. Not the people who have it figured out. The brokenhearted. The crushed in spirit. If you are in this room, you may qualify. What does it mean that brokenness is not a barrier to God's nearness — but may be the very thing that draws Him close?

The Two Tracks

Track A — For the One in the Struggle

A1. Chapter 1 describes the moment of crisis — when the floor drops out. You may be at the beginning of this journey, or you may be well into it. Either way, Psalm 23:4 says the valley has a "through." Do you believe that right now? Be honest. You don't have to feel it yet. But what would it mean if it were true?

A2. James says the testing of your faith produces endurance. You may not have asked for this test. But you are in it. What would endurance look like for you — not in six months, but this week?

A3. Psalm 34:18 says the Lord is near to the brokenhearted. Not near to the people who have cleaned themselves up. Not near to the people who have it together. Near to the broken. Are you willing to let yourself be broken before God — honestly, without performance — and let that be the starting point?

Track B — For the Family

B1. You may have received your own "phone call" — the moment the crisis became real. Psalm 23:4 does not say the valley is only for the person struggling. The family walks through it too. Where are you in the valley right now? And what does it mean to you that it has a "through"?

B2. James 1:2-4 says to consider it joy when you encounter trials — because the testing produces endurance. That is hard to hear when your child, your spouse, your sibling is destroying themselves. James is not being dismissive. He is saying: this will produce something in you, if you let it. What might God be producing in you through this trial — even though you didn't ask for it?

B3. Psalm 34:18 — "The LORD is near to the brokenhearted." You may have been so focused on your loved one's brokenness that you haven't acknowledged your own. The Lord is near to *you* too. What would it look like to bring your own broken heart to God this week, instead of carrying it alone?

Memory Verse

"Even though I walk through the valley of the shadow of death, I fear no evil, for You are with me."

— Psalm 23:4 (NASB)

For the Week Ahead

This week, read Psalm 23 once each day. The whole psalm — all six verses. It takes less than a minute. Don't study it. Don't analyze it. Read it the way a person reads a letter from someone who loves them. Let it settle. You are in the valley. The Shepherd is with you. And the valley has a *through*.

THE PROGRESSION

Chapter 2 — "The Progression"

Before the Group Meets

Read Chapter 2 of *Change the Mind, Change the Man.*

Then read:

- **Romans 1:18-25**
- **James 1:13-16**
- **Romans 6:16**
- **Proverbs 13:20**

Opening

Have someone read James 1:14-15 aloud.

> *"But each one is tempted when he is carried away and enticed by his own lust. Then when lust has conceived, it gives birth to sin; and when sin is accomplished, it brings forth death."*

Then ask: **How many steps are in this progression?**

James describes a sequence, not an event. Desire. Enticement. Conception. Sin. Death. Nobody starts at the end. Everyone starts at the first step — and nobody taking that first step believes they will end up at the last one. That is how progression works. And James described it two thousand years before anyone used the word "addiction."

Into the Text

Passage 1 — Romans 1:18-25

(Have someone read the full passage aloud.)

1. Verse 21 says "even though they knew God, they did not honor Him as God or give thanks." The turning does not begin with ignorance. It begins with *knowing* God and choosing not to honor Him. Why is that distinction important? What does it mean that the progression begins not in darkness but in light that is deliberately turned away from?

2. Follow the sequence Paul traces: they knew God (v. 21) → they did not honor Him (v. 21) → they became futile in their speculations (v. 21) → their heart was darkened (v. 21) → they exchanged the glory of God (v. 23) → God gave them over (v. 24). How many of those steps are *choices*, and how many are *consequences*? Where does the choosing stop and the consequences begin?

3. Verse 25 says they "exchanged the truth of God for a lie, and worshiped and served the creature rather than the Creator." The book argues that when the mind drifts from God, the self fills the vacuum, and the substance fills the emptiness the self creates. Read verse 25 again with that framework in mind. What was exchanged? And what was received in its place?

Passage 2 — James 1:13-16

> *"Let no one say when he is tempted, 'I am being tempted by God'; for God cannot be tempted by evil, and He Himself does not tempt anyone. But each one is tempted when he is carried away and enticed by his own lust. Then when lust has conceived, it gives birth to sin; and when sin is accomplished, it brings forth death. Do not be deceived, my beloved brethren."*

Questions:

4. Verse 13 eliminates one excuse: "God made me this way" or "God put me in this situation." James shuts that door. Where does the temptation come from, according to verse 14? What does that do to the argument that addiction is someone else's fault?

5. James uses the language of pregnancy and birth: desire *conceives*, sin is *born*, death is *brought forth*. Why does James use that imagery? What does it tell you about how sin develops — is it sudden, or does it grow?

6. Verse 16 says "do not be deceived." The entire progression James has just described is itself a deception. At every stage, the person believes the next step will satisfy, will be manageable, will be the last. Where have you seen that deception at work?

Passage 3 — Romans 6:16

"Do you not know that when you present yourselves to someone as slaves for obedience, you are slaves of the one whom you obey, either of sin resulting in death, or of obedience resulting in righteousness?"

Questions:

7. Paul says you become a *slave* of what you obey. Not a casual participant. A slave. The word means you no longer belong to yourself. How does this verse describe the experience of addiction — even though Paul is writing about sin in general, not substances in particular?

8. Notice that Paul presents only two options: slavery to sin, or obedience resulting in righteousness. There is no neutral ground — no category for "I can handle it" or "I'm in control." Why does that matter for someone in the early stages of the progression?

Passage 4 — Proverbs 13:20

"He who walks with wise men will be wise, but the companion of fools will suffer harm."

Questions:

9. This is a proverb — a general principle of wisdom. It does not say "might suffer harm." It says "will suffer harm." The book describes how the people you associate with change during the progression of addiction. According to this verse, that change of company is not neutral. It is directional. What direction does it go?

The Two Tracks

Track A — For the One in the Struggle

A1. James 1:14-15 traces a progression: desire → enticement → sin → death. Think about your own story honestly. Can you identify the stages? Where was the first step — not the worst step, but the *first* one?

A2. Romans 1:21 says the turning began when people who *knew* God chose not to honor Him. Was there a time when you knew what was right and turned away from it anyway? What did you tell yourself to make that turn feel acceptable?

A3. Romans 6:16 says you are a slave of what you obey. Be honest with yourself: right now, what are you obeying? And what does Paul say that obedience leads to?

A4. Proverbs 13:20 says the companion of fools will suffer harm. When the chapter describes the changed associations — the old friends replaced by new ones — did you recognize your own story? What would it mean to begin changing the company you keep again, this time in the other direction?

Track B — For the Family

B1. Romans 1:21-25 describes a progression of exchange — trading truth for lies, glory for shame, the Creator for the creation. You may have watched this progression happen in someone you love. The hardest part is that you could see it and they could not. What does this passage tell you about why they couldn't see it — and why your seeing it was not enough to stop it?

B2. James 1:14 says each person is carried away "by his own lust." The word "own" is doing essential work. The desire belongs to the individual. It does not belong to the family. You did not create the desire. You did not plant it. This is not a verse about what you did wrong. It is a verse about where the responsibility lies. Does that bring you any relief? Be honest.

B3. Proverbs 13:20 says the companion of fools will suffer harm. You are suffering harm — not because you are foolish, but because someone you love made foolish choices, and the harm radiates outward. The proverb describes a reality. It does not say you deserved it. How do you carry the harm of someone else's choices without being destroyed by it? (You don't have to answer that fully this week. But sit with the question.)

Memory Verse

> *"But each one is tempted when he is carried away and enticed by his own lust. Then when lust has conceived, it gives birth to sin; and when sin is accomplished, it brings forth death."*
>
> — James 1:14-15 (NASB)

For the Week Ahead

Read Romans 1:21-25 once this week. Read it slowly. Notice the exchange — the trade. Truth for a lie. The glory of God for something less. Then ask yourself — not with guilt, but with honesty — what trades have been made in your life? What was given up, and what was received in its place? You don't have to fix anything this week. Just see it clearly.

WHERE DID WE GO WRONG?

Chapter 3 — "Where Did We Go Wrong?"

Before the Group Meets

Read Chapter 3 of *Change the Mind, Change the Man.*

Then read:

- **Ezekiel 18:1-4, 19-20**
- **Proverbs 22:6**
- **Proverbs 17:21, 25**
- **Deuteronomy 24:16**

Opening

Have someone read Ezekiel 18:20 aloud.

> *"The person who sins will die. The son will not bear the punishment for the father's iniquity, nor will the father bear the punishment for the son's iniquity; the righteousness of the righteous will be upon himself, and the wickedness of the wicked will be upon himself."*

Then ask: **Who bears the responsibility for sin, according to this verse?**

This is one of the clearest statements in all of Scripture about personal accountability. The son does not bear the father's guilt. The father does not bear the son's guilt. Each person stands before God on the basis of their own choices. This verse does two things at once: it places the weight of responsibility squarely on the one who sinned, and it lifts a burden that many families have been carrying that was never theirs to carry.

Into the Text

Passage 1 — Ezekiel 18:1-4, 19-20

(Have someone read both sections aloud.)

Questions:

1. In verses 1-3, God addresses a proverb the people of Israel were repeating: "The fathers eat the sour grapes, but the children's teeth are set on edge." What does that proverb claim? And what does God say about it? (Look at verse 3 carefully — "you are surely not going to use this proverb in Israel anymore.")

2. Verse 4 says "all souls are Mine." Before God addresses the question of responsibility, He establishes ownership. Every soul belongs to Him — the father's and the son's. Why does that matter as the foundation for what follows?

3. In verse 20, the statement is absolute: the son will not bear the father's punishment, and the father will not bear the son's. If this is true — and God says it is — what does that mean for the parent who has been asking "Where did we go wrong?" Does this verse answer that question? How?

4. Does this verse remove *all* parental responsibility, or does it specifically address *guilt for the child's sin*? There is a difference between "I failed as a parent" and "I am guilty of my child's sin." Ezekiel addresses the second. What does honest self-examination look like for a parent without crossing into carrying guilt that God says is not theirs?

Passage 2 — Proverbs 22:6

"Train up a child in the way he should go, even when he is old he will not depart from it."

Questions:

5. This verse has been used to comfort parents — and to condemn them. If the child departs, the reasoning goes, the training must have failed. But is that what the verse says? Proverbs are wisdom literature — they describe how life generally works, not unconditional guarantees. How do we know this? Because the same book of Proverbs acknowledges the possibility of a foolish son (Proverbs 17:25). Can both verses be true? How?

6. If Proverbs 22:6 were an unconditional promise, what would that do to the child's free will? Could a person truly choose to reject God if their parents' faithfulness guaranteed they would not?

Passage 3 — Deuteronomy 24:16

"Fathers shall not be put to death for their sons, nor shall sons be put to death for their fathers; everyone shall be put to death for his own sin."

Questions:

7. This is a legal statute in Israel's law — God's rule for how justice was administered. Each person was held accountable for their own sin, not their family's. Taken together with Ezekiel 18:20, what principle is God establishing about individual accountability? And how does that principle apply to the way we think about addiction and the family?

The Two Tracks

Track A — For the One in the Struggle

A1. Ezekiel 18:20 says the wickedness of the wicked is upon himself. That means your choices belong to you. Not to your parents, not to your circumstances, not to the people who introduced you to the substance. You. Is that hard to hear — or is it actually liberating? Because if the choice was yours, the turning is also yours.

A2. Some people blame their upbringing for their addiction. Some of those people are right that their upbringing was broken. But Ezekiel does not say "the son will not bear the father's punishment unless the father was really bad." The principle stands regardless. Your father's failures — real or imagined — do not own your choices. How does that change the way you think about your own responsibility?

A3. Proverbs 22:6 says to train up a child in the way he should go. Were you trained? Was there a foundation — even one you walked away from? If there was, it may still be there. Foundations do not disappear just because someone builds something else on top of them. Is there a foundation in your past that you abandoned but did not destroy?

Track B — For the Family

B1. Ezekiel 18:20. Read it one more time. "The father will not bear the punishment for the son's iniquity." God said that. Not a counselor. Not a well-meaning friend. God. If you have been carrying the guilt of your loved one's choices — if you have been asking "Where did we go wrong?" as if the answer is that *you* are the reason — this verse is God lifting that weight off of you. Can you let Him?

B2. Proverbs 22:6 may have been used against you — by others or by yourself. "If you had trained them right, this wouldn't have happened." But the same book of wisdom says "a foolish son is a grief to his father and bitterness to her who bore him" (17:25). Solomon, the wisest man who ever lived, wrote that. The existence of foolish children is not evidence of failed parenting. It is evidence of human free will. How does that reframe the guilt you have been carrying?

B3. Honesty check: some families did fail in real ways. Absent parents. Broken homes. Harmful environments. If that is your story, Ezekiel does not give you an excuse — but it gives your child no excuse either. And it gives you a path forward: each soul stands on its own before God. Your failures are yours to bring before God. Your child's choices are theirs. What does repentance look like for you — not for their sin, but for your own?

Memory Verse

"The person who sins will die. The son will not bear the punishment for the father's iniquity, nor will the father bear the punishment for the son's iniquity."

— Ezekiel 18:20 (NASB)

For the Week Ahead

If you are a parent or a family member, read Ezekiel 18:20 once each morning this week. Every time the guilt rises — every time "Where did we go wrong?" starts replaying — read the verse again. Let God's word answer the question you have been asking yourself. The son's sin is the son's. The father's sin is the father's. Each soul belongs to God. Each soul answers to God.

If you are the one in the struggle, read it too. Because it means your choices are yours. And if they are yours, you can make different ones.

ALL OF THE IMPRISONED AREN'T IN PRISON

Chapter 4 — "All of the Imprisoned Aren't in Prison"

Before the Group Meets

Read Chapter 4 of *Change the Mind, Change the Man.*

Then read:

- **John 8:31-36**
- **2 Peter 2:19**
- **James 5:16**
- **Galatians 6:1-2**

Opening

Have someone read John 8:34 aloud.

> *"Jesus answered them, 'Truly, truly, I say to you, everyone who commits sin is the slave of sin.'"*

Then ask: **Who is "everyone"?**

Jesus does not say "the person who commits a lot of sin" or "the person who commits the worst sins." He says *everyone* who commits sin is the slave of sin. That includes the person chained to a substance. It also includes the person who has never touched an illegal drug but is enslaved to something else — anger, pornography, bitterness, the approval of others. The prisons are not all made of concrete and steel. Some of them have nice furniture.

Into the Text

Passage 1 — John 8:31-36

(Have someone read the full passage aloud.)

Questions:

1. In verse 31, Jesus says "if you continue in My word, then you are truly disciples of Mine." What does it mean to *continue* in His word? Is this a one-time event, or an ongoing practice? Why does that distinction matter for someone trying to break free from any form of slavery?

2. Verse 32: "You will know the truth, and the truth will make you free." The people Jesus is speaking to respond in verse 33: "We have never been enslaved to anyone." They could not see their own chains. How common is it for people to deny that they are enslaved — not just to substances, but to anything that has mastered them?

3. Verse 34 — "everyone who commits sin is the slave of sin." And then verse 36 — "So if the Son makes you free, you will be free indeed." Jesus identifies the slavery *and* the only source of genuine freedom in the same conversation. Where does the freedom come from? Not from willpower. Not from a change of environment. From whom?

Passage 2 — 2 Peter 2:19

"Promising them freedom while they themselves are slaves of corruption; for by what a man is overcome, by this he is enslaved."

Questions:

4. Peter says that people can *promise* freedom while being slaves themselves. What does that look like in the context of addiction? Think about the false promises — "I can stop whenever I want," "This time will be different," "One more time won't hurt." Who is making those promises? And are they free?

5. "By what a man is overcome, by this he is enslaved." This is a definition of slavery that has nothing to do with iron chains. It is about being *overcome*. What overcomes a person? And what does it mean that the thing that overcomes you is the thing that owns you?

Passage 3 — James 5:16

"Therefore, confess your sins to one another, and pray for one another so that you may be healed. The effective prayer of a righteous man can accomplish much."

Questions:

6. The book argues that addiction thrives in secrecy — that hiding IS the progression continuing. James connects confession, prayer, and healing in a single verse. Why does James put *confession* first? What does secrecy protect — and what does it prevent?

7. James says to confess "to one another." This requires community. It requires trust. It requires a group of people who will not weaponize your honesty. What kind of environment does this verse assume? And what is the church's responsibility in creating that environment?

Passage 4 — Galatians 6:1-2

"Brethren, even if anyone is caught in any trespass, you who are spiritual, restore such a one in a spirit of gentleness; each one looking to yourself, so that you too will not be tempted. Bear one another's burdens, and thereby fulfill the law of Christ."

Questions:

8. Paul says to restore the one caught in trespass "in a spirit of gentleness." Not in a spirit of condemnation. Not with an air of superiority. Gentleness. And then he adds a warning: "each one looking to yourself, so that you too will not be tempted." Why does Paul add that warning? What does it prevent?

9. "Bear one another's burdens." This is a command, not a suggestion. What does it look like for the body of Christ to actually bear the burden of a family dealing with addiction? And what happens when the church refuses to?

The Two Tracks

Track A — For the One in the Struggle

A1. John 8:34 — "everyone who commits sin is the slave of sin." Can you name your slavery honestly? Not in vague terms. Specifically. What has overcome you? What owns you right now?

A2. 2 Peter 2:19 says you are enslaved by what overcomes you. But John 8:36 says the Son can set you free — "free indeed." Not partially free. Not free with conditions. Free *indeed*. Do you believe that is possible for you? What stands between you and believing it?

A3. James 5:16 says to confess your sins to one another. Is there anyone in your life you have been honest with — truly honest? If not, what is the secrecy protecting? And what is it costing you?

Track B — For the Family

B1. The chapter describes hidden prisons: the wife who can't tell anyone at church, the parents smiling on Sunday and falling apart on Monday, the family hiding from everyone. Are you in a hidden prison? James 5:16 says confession and prayer lead to healing. That is not just for the addict. It is for you. What would it look like to tell someone the truth about what you are going through?

B2. Galatians 6:1-2 describes what the church is supposed to do when someone is caught in a trespass. "Restore... in a spirit of gentleness." "Bear one another's burdens." Has the church been that for you? If not, what did you receive instead? And what should you have received, according to this text?

B3. John 8:32 — "the truth will make you free." You may be imprisoned by the secret. You may be imprisoned by fear of judgment. You may be imprisoned by the exhaustion of pretending. The truth — spoken to the right people, in the right setting — is the beginning of freedom. Not just for the addict. For you.

Memory Verse

"So if the Son makes you free, you will be free indeed."

— John 8:36 (NASB)

For the Week Ahead

This week, ask yourself one honest question each day: *What has mastered me?* Not just substances. Anything. Fear. Anger. The need for control. The need to fix someone. Bitterness. Whatever it is — name it. Not to beat yourself up. To see it clearly. Because John 8:36 says the Son can set you free. But you have to know what you need freeing from.

LOVE THAT SAYS NO

Chapter 5 — "Love That Says No"

Before the Group Meets

Read Chapter 5 of *Change the Mind, Change the Man.*

Then read:

- **1 Corinthians 5:1-8, 13**
- **2 Corinthians 2:5-11**
- **Hebrews 12:5-11**
- **Luke 15:12-16** (just the departure and the consequences — not the return yet)

Opening

Have someone read 1 Corinthians 5:5 aloud.

> *"I have decided to deliver such a one to Satan for the destruction of his flesh, so that his spirit may be saved in the day of the Lord Jesus."*

Then ask: **What is the purpose of the removal?**

Read the end of the verse again: "so that his spirit may be saved." The removal was not punishment for punishment's sake. It was not vengeance. It was the most severe act of love the church could perform — removing a man from the fellowship so that the shock of being outside might awaken him to what he was losing. The purpose was *redemptive*. This is what love looks like when every other option has been exhausted.

Into the Text

Passage 1 — 1 Corinthians 5:1-8, 13

Questions:

1. Paul says the Corinthian church was *proud* instead of mourning (verse 2). They were tolerating the sin rather than addressing it. Why is tolerance of destructive behavior not the same as love? What is the difference between accepting a person and accepting what is destroying them?

2. The instruction is to "remove the wicked man from among yourselves" (verse 13). This is not gentle. It is not comfortable. But verse 5 gives the reason — "so that his spirit may be saved." Can an act of removal be an act of love? What makes it love rather than abandonment? (Hint: look at the purpose.)

3. In verse 6, Paul says "a little leaven leavens the whole lump." What is being protected by the removal — only the man being removed, or also the community? How does this apply to a family's decision to set boundaries with an addicted family member?

Passage 2 — 2 Corinthians 2:5-11

Questions:

4. Most scholars believe this is the same man from 1 Corinthians 5 — now repentant. What does Paul instruct the church to do now? (Look at verses 7-8: "forgive and comfort him... reaffirm your love for him.") What does this tell you about the other side of "love that says no"? The removal was not permanent. The goal was always restoration.

5. Verse 7 says to forgive and comfort "so that he will not be overwhelmed by excessive sorrow." Paul is concerned about going too far the other direction — making restoration so punitive that it crushes the person. What does this balance look like practically? How do you hold both the boundary (1 Corinthians 5) and the restoration (2 Corinthians 2) together?

Passage 3 — Hebrews 12:5-11

Questions:

6. Verse 6: "For those whom the Lord loves He disciplines, and He scourges every son whom He receives." God disciplines those He *loves*. If the Father Himself loves through discipline, what does that tell us about whether discipline can be an act of love?

7. Verse 11: "All discipline for the moment seems not to be joyful, but sorrowful; yet to those who have been trained by it, afterwards it yields the peaceful fruit of righteousness." The key word is "afterwards." Discipline does not feel like love in the moment. It feels like pain. But "afterwards" it yields something. What does it yield? And what does that tell the family who fears that setting a boundary will destroy the relationship?

Passage 4 — Luke 15:12-16

(Have someone read aloud. Stop at verse 16 — do not read the return yet. That comes in Week 7.)

Questions:

8. The father in Luke 15 gives the son what he asks for — his inheritance — and lets him go. He does not chase him. He does not fund the trip. He does not send money when the son runs out. The son ends up in a pig pen, longing to eat the pods the pigs ate. Sometimes love lets someone hit the bottom. Why did the father not intervene? And what happened *because* he didn't? (Look ahead to verse 17 — "he came to his senses." That coming to his senses required the pig pen.)

The Two Tracks

Track A — For the One in the Struggle

A1. Has someone in your life set a boundary with you — refused to give you money, refused to let you come home, refused to cover for you? At the time, did it feel like love or like abandonment? Read 1 Corinthians 5:5 again — "so that his spirit may be saved." Is it possible that the person who said no to you was loving you more than the person who kept saying yes?

A2. Hebrews 12:11 says discipline "afterwards yields the peaceful fruit of righteousness." Have you experienced any "afterwards" yet? Or are you still in the "for the moment" — the part that seems sorrowful? If you are still in the sorrowful part, what would it take to trust that there is an "afterwards"?

A3. The prodigal son had to reach the pig pen before he came to his senses. Had anyone rescued him before that point, he would never have turned around. Where are you in the story? And is someone trying to rescue you from the very thing that might be the turning point?

Track B — For the Family

B1. This is the hardest chapter for families. 1 Corinthians 5 describes the church removing a man — and Paul says it was the right thing to do. But the purpose was redemptive, not punitive. When you set a boundary, what is your purpose? Punishment? Self-protection? Love? Be honest — because the purpose is what separates a closed door from an abandoned person.

B2. Hebrews 12:6 — "those whom the Lord loves He disciplines." You may feel guilty for setting boundaries. You may feel like you are failing your loved one. But if God Himself disciplines those He loves, then discipline is not a failure of love. It is an expression of it. Can you hold that truth this week, even when the guilt returns?

B3. Read 2 Corinthians 2:5-11. The same church that removed the man was told to receive him back when he repented — with forgiveness, comfort, and reaffirmed love. The boundary was not forever. It was until. Are you holding a boundary right now? Is it a boundary with a purpose — with an "until" — or has it become permanent rejection? There is a difference. And Scripture holds both the firmness and the restoration together.

B4. The chapter warns against checklists — every situation is different. Wisdom is required, not formulas. If you are facing a decision about boundaries right now, bring it to the text, bring it to prayer, and bring it to wise, mature Christians who will be honest with you. Do not carry this decision alone.

Memory Verse

> *"For those whom the Lord loves He disciplines, and He scourges every son whom He receives."*
> — Hebrews 12:6 (NASB)

For the Week Ahead

This week, read Hebrews 12:5-11 once. Then sit with this question: Is there a boundary you need to set — or a boundary you need to maintain — that you have been afraid to hold? Or is there a boundary that has become punishment rather than love, and needs to be reconsidered?

You don't have to act this week. But let the text speak to the question. And pray for the wisdom James 1:5 says God gives generously to those who ask.

THINK

Chapter 6 — "Think"

Before the Group Meets

Read Chapter 6 of *Change the Mind, Change the Man.*

Then read the following passages — slowly, more than once — before you come to the group:

- **Romans 12:1-2**
- **Philippians 2:1-8**
- **Philippians 4:8**
- **Colossians 3:1-4**

That's your preparation. Read the chapter. Then sit with those four passages. When you come to the group, come ready to talk about what *they* say — not what you think about them, but what they actually say.

Opening

Have someone read Romans 12:1-2 aloud to the group.

Then ask: **What does Paul say is the mechanism of transformation?**

Don't rush past the answer. It's right there in the text. The transformation Paul calls for is not a transformation of behavior first — it is a transformation of the *mind.* "Be transformed by the renewing of your mind." Everything else follows from that.

This is the hinge of the entire book, and it is the hinge of this study. Every chapter before this one traced how the mind turns away from God. Every chapter after this one traces what happens when it turns back. This week, we sit with the turning itself.

Into the Text

Passage 1 — Romans 12:1-2

"Therefore I urge you, brethren, by the mercies of God, to present your bodies a living and holy sacrifice, acceptable to God, which is your spiritual service of worship. And do not be conformed to this world, but be transformed by the renewing of your mind, so that you may prove what the will of God is, that which is good and acceptable and perfect."

Questions:

1. Paul says "do not be conformed" and "be transformed." What is the difference between being *conformed* to something and being *transformed*? One is being shaped from the outside in; the other is being changed from the inside out. Which one describes what the world does to a person? Which one describes what God does?

2. The word translated "transformed" is the Greek word *metamorphoō* — the same word that gives us "metamorphosis." A caterpillar does not put on a butterfly costume. It becomes a different creature entirely. What does that tell you about the kind of change Paul is describing?

3. Where does the transformation begin, according to this passage? Not in the hands. Not in the habits. It begins in the *mind*. Why does that matter for someone trying to overcome addiction? Why does it matter for someone watching a loved one try?

4. Paul does not say "be transformed by willpower" or "be transformed by a change of scenery." He says "by the renewing of your mind." What renews a mind? Where does the new way of thinking come from?

Passage 2 — Philippians 2:1-8

(Have someone read aloud.)

Questions:

5. In verse 2, Paul uses four phrases to describe unity: "same mind," "same love," "united in spirit," "intent on one purpose." How many of those four are about how a person *thinks*?

6. Verse 3 says "do nothing from selfishness." The book argues that when the mind drifts from God, the self fills the vacuum. Read verse 3 again with that in mind. What is the opposite of selfishness according to this verse? And what does that require the mind to be doing?

7. Verse 5 says to have the same *mind* as Christ. Then verses 6-8 describe what that mind looked like in action. Christ did not grasp. He emptied. He served. He obeyed. What kind of thinking produces that kind of living?

Passage 3 — Colossians 3:1-4

(Have someone read aloud.)

Questions:

8. "Set your mind on the things above, not on the things that are on earth." This is a command. The word implies a deliberate, sustained act of the will. What does it look like, practically, to set your mind on something? And what happens when you don't — when the mind has no fixed point?

9. The book's thesis is that the gaze was the real problem — not the substance. Read verse 2 again with that in mind. If the mind is set on "things above," what is it *not* set on?

Passage 4 — Philippians 4:8

(Have someone read aloud.)

Questions:

10. Look at the list: true, honorable, right, pure, lovely, of good repute, excellent, worthy of praise. These are not random qualities. They describe God and the things of God. What happens to a person's mind — over time — when it is filled with these things?

11. The word translated "dwell on" is the Greek *logizomai*. It means to calculate, to reckon, to take careful account of. It is not casual. It is deliberate, sustained, focused attention. Why would Paul choose a word that means *calculate* rather than a word that means *consider*?

12. Read this verse in light of everything you've read today — Romans 12:1-2, Philippians 2:1-8, Colossians 3:1-4. This is not one verse about positive thinking. This is the capstone of an entire theology of the mind. What are you filling your mind with? And is it any of these things?

The Two Tracks

Track A — For the One in the Struggle

A1. The book says: "No program, no facility, no change of environment will hold if your mind doesn't change." Looking back at your own attempts to change, was it your *circumstances* that changed, or was it your *mind*?

A2. Romans 12:2 says the mind is renewed. It does not say the mind renews itself. Where is the renewal coming from? What does that mean for someone who has tried — and failed — to change by sheer determination?

A3. Colossians 3:2 commands you to set your mind on things above. Be specific: what occupied your mind before? What would it look like — tomorrow morning, not in theory — to begin setting it somewhere else?

A4. Philippians 4:8 gives you a list. True. Honorable. Right. Pure. When your mind is not on these things, what is it on instead? Name it honestly, at least to yourself.

Track B — For the Family

B1. Chapter 6 says you cannot change your loved one's mind for them. Read Romans 12:1-2. Who does the urging? Who does the presenting? What does that tell you about the limits of what you can do for someone else — and about the One who is still at work even when you can't be?

B2. Your mind needs renewing too. Fear, guilt, anger, replaying every memory — these are the thought patterns that imprison families. Philippians 4:8 is not only for the addict. What have you been dwelling on? And what does the text say to dwell on instead?

B3. Philippians 2:3-4 describes both humility and obedience to the Father's will. How does the "mind of Christ" help you distinguish between self-sacrificing love and destructive enabling?

B4. Colossians 3:2 — "Set your mind on the things above." When the crisis is consuming, "things above" can feel impossibly far away. What is one thing from this week's study that you can set your mind on when the fear takes over?

Memory Verse

"And do not be conformed to this world, but be transformed by the renewing of your mind, so that you may prove what the will of God is, that which is good and acceptable and perfect."

— Romans 12:2 (NASB)

For the Week Ahead

Each day this week, before anything else occupies your mind, read Philippians 4:8 once. Then ask yourself honestly what your mind was set on yesterday. You don't have to write anything down. You don't have to report to anyone. Just read the verse. Ask the question. Let the text do what the text does.

PART TWO

THE RETURN: THE MIND TURNING BACK

COMING TO HIMSELF

Chapter 7 — "Coming to Himself"

Before the Group Meets

Read Chapter 7 of *Change the Mind, Change the Man.*

Then read:

- **Luke 15:11-24** (the full prodigal son account through the father's response)
- **Psalm 51:1-17**
- **James 4:13-17**
- **Romans 7:15-25**

Opening

Have someone read Luke 15:17 aloud.

> *"But when he came to his senses, he said, 'How many of my father's hired men have more than enough bread, but I am dying here with hunger!'"*

Then ask: **What had to happen before he came to his senses?**

Look at what came before verse 17. He had spent everything (v. 14). A famine came (v. 14). He attached himself to a citizen of that country and was sent to feed pigs (v. 15). He longed to fill himself with the pods the pigs ate, and no one gave him anything (v. 16). He had to reach the absolute end of himself before his mind turned. The pig pen was not the punishment. The pig pen was the classroom. It was where the thinking finally changed.

Into the Text

Passage 1 — Luke 15:17-20a

"But when he came to his senses, he said, 'How many of my father's hired men have more than enough bread, but I am dying here with hunger! I will get up and go to my father, and will say to him, "Father, I have sinned against heaven, and in your sight; I am no longer worthy to be called your son; make me as one of your hired men."' And he got up and came to his father."

Questions:

1. "He came to his senses." Other translations say "he came to himself." The idea is that he had been outside of his right mind and now returned to clear thinking. What does that tell you about the state of mind during the progression of addiction? And what does it tell you about what repentance actually is — a return to right thinking?

2. Look at what the son says in verse 18: "I have sinned against heaven, and in your sight." He names it. He does not say "mistakes were made." He does not blame his brother, the famine, or the citizen who sent him to the pig pen. He takes ownership. Why is that essential to genuine repentance?

3. Verse 18 says he sinned "against heaven" first, and then "in your sight." The sin against God comes before the sin against the father. Why does the order matter?

4. Verse 20 says "he got up and came." He did not just think about it. He did not plan to do it tomorrow. He got up. What is the difference between remorse and repentance, according to this verse?

Passage 2 — Psalm 51:1-4, 10, 16-17

(Have someone read these selected verses aloud.)

Questions:

5. David wrote Psalm 51 after his sin with Bathsheba and the murder of Uriah. Verse 3: "I know my transgressions, and my sin is ever before me." Verse 4: "Against You, You only, I have sinned and done what is evil in Your sight." David sinned against many people — Bathsheba, Uriah, the nation. Yet he says "against You only." What does David understand about the nature of sin that the prodigal also understood?

6. Verse 10: "Create in me a clean heart, O God, and renew a steadfast spirit within me." David asks God to *create* — the Hebrew word is *bara*, the same word used in Genesis 1:1.

David is not asking for a tune-up. He is asking for a new creation. What does that tell you about the magnitude of the change he needs?

7. Verses 16-17: "For You do not delight in sacrifice, otherwise I would give it; You are not pleased with burnt offering. The sacrifices of God are a broken spirit; a broken and a contrite heart, O God, You will not despise." What does God want from the one who has sinned? Not a performance. Not a ritual. A broken and contrite heart. What is the difference between performing repentance and being broken by it?

Passage 3 — James 4:13-17

(Have someone read aloud.)

Questions:

8. Verse 14: "You do not know what your life will be like tomorrow. You are just a vapor that appears for a little while and then vanishes away." The book describes the folly of waiting — "I'll turn back to God when I get out," "I'll deal with it later." What does James say about the assumption that tomorrow is guaranteed?

9. Verse 17: "To one who knows the right thing to do and does not do it, to him it is sin." If you know what needs to change — if the previous six weeks of study have made it clear — what does this verse say about waiting?

Passage 4 — Romans 7:15-20

(Have someone read aloud.)

Questions:

10. Paul writes: "For what I am doing, I do not understand; for I am not practicing what I would like to do, but I am doing the very thing I hate." Every person who has struggled with addiction knows this war. Paul the apostle knew it too. What does it mean that this war is not unique to addiction — that it is the universal human struggle with sin?

11. Verse 24: "Wretched man that I am! Who will set me free from the body of this death?" Paul does not answer with a program. He answers with a Person — verse 25: "Thanks be to God through Jesus Christ our Lord!" Where does the deliverance come from?

The Two Tracks

Track A — For the One in the Struggle

A1. The prodigal "came to his senses." Have you? Be honest. Are you in the pig pen and still making excuses, or have you reached the point where you are ready to say, "I have sinned against heaven"? There is no shame in admitting you are not there yet. But there is danger in pretending you are when you are not.

A2. The difference between remorse and repentance is the difference between "I'm sorry I got caught" and "I have sinned against heaven." Which one describes you right now? Your family has probably seen the first one before. Maybe many times. What would the second one look like — genuinely?

A3. James 4:14 says you do not know what your life will be like tomorrow. You may be waiting for a better time, a more convenient moment, a change of circumstances. What if that moment doesn't come? What does the text say about waiting?

A4. Romans 7:15 — "I am doing the very thing I hate." You know this war. Paul knew it too. And his answer was not a strategy. It was a Person. Who sets you free?

Track B — For the Family

B1. You may have seen false repentance before — the tears, the promises, the temporary change followed by the same behavior. Psalm 51 shows what real repentance looks like: specific confession (v. 3-4), acknowledgment that the sin is against God (v. 4), a plea for God to create something new (v. 10), a broken spirit rather than a performance (v. 17). How does this help you recognize the real thing — and how does it help you extend grace when you see it?

B2. You desperately want your loved one to "come to his senses." But you cannot come to their senses for them. The prodigal had to reach the pig pen. The father had to let him go there. What does it mean to wait — not passively, not helplessly, but with the kind of trust that the father had when he let his son walk out the door?

B3. James 4:14 applies to you too. You may be waiting for them to change before you address your own spiritual needs. But your life is also a vapor. What does your own walk with God look like right now — apart from the crisis? Have you neglected it? And what does James 4:17 say about knowing what you ought to do?

Memory Verse

"But when he came to his senses, he said, 'How many of my father's hired men have more than enough bread, but I am dying here with hunger! I will get up and go to my father.'"

— Luke 15:17-18a (NASB)

For the Week Ahead

Read Psalm 51 once this week — the whole psalm. Read it as David's prayer. Then read it as your own. Wherever the words fit — "I know my transgressions," "against You only I have sinned," "create in me a clean heart" — let them be yours. This is not someone else's prayer. This is the prayer of anyone who has reached the place where honesty is the only option left.

THE FATHER RAN

Chapter 8 — "The Father Ran"

Before the Group Meets

Read Chapter 8 of *Change the Mind, Change the Man.*

Then read:

- **Luke 15:20-32** (finish the parable)
- **2 Samuel 12:1-14**
- **Psalm 51:1-4, 10-13**
- **2 Corinthians 2:5-11**

Opening

Have someone read Luke 15:20 aloud.

> *"So he got up and came to his father. But while he was still a long way off, his father saw him and felt compassion for him, and ran and embraced him and kissed him."*

Then ask: **What was the father doing that allowed him to see his son "a long way off"?**

He was watching. He had been watching. The text does not say how long. But the father saw him while he was still far away, which means the father had never stopped looking toward the road. And when he saw him, he did not wait for the son to arrive. He did not stand at the door with his arms crossed. He ran. In the ancient Near Eastern world, a dignified man did not run. The father abandoned his dignity for his son. That is grace.

Into the Text

Passage 1 — Luke 15:20-24

(Have someone read aloud.)

Questions:

1. The son begins his prepared speech in verse 21: "Father, I have sinned against heaven and in your sight; I am no longer worthy to be called your son." But notice — the father interrupts him. He never lets the son finish the speech. Look at verse 22: "the father said to his slaves, 'Quickly bring out the best robe and put it on him.'" What does that tell you about what the father was looking for? Was he waiting for the right words — or for the right direction of travel?

2. The robe, the ring, the sandals, the fattened calf — each one means something. The robe is honor. The ring is authority. The sandals are the mark of a son, not a slave (slaves went barefoot). The feast is celebration. The father does not restore the son halfway. He restores him fully. What does full restoration look like — and what does it *not* look like? (Note: the inheritance is gone. It is not returned. Restoration does not mean consequences disappear.)

3. Verse 24: "This son of mine was dead and has come to life again; he was lost and has been found." The father uses the language of death and resurrection. Not "he made a mistake and corrected it." Dead and alive. Lost and found. Why does the father use such extreme language?

Passage 2 — Luke 15:25-32 — The Older Brother

(Have someone read aloud.)

Questions:

4. The older brother is angry (v. 28). He refuses to go in. He says, "I have been serving you" (v. 29) — and notice the bitterness in it. "You have never given me a young goat" (v. 29). He has been keeping score. What does the older brother's response tell you about a different kind of imprisoned thinking — one that looks righteous on the outside?

5. The father says to the older brother, "Son, you have always been with me, and all that is mine is yours" (v. 31). The older brother's inheritance was never at risk. His place was never in question. But he could not celebrate his brother's return because he was consumed by what he felt he was owed. Where do you see the older brother in the story of addiction — in the family, in the church, or even in yourself?

6. Jesus leaves the parable without resolving the older brother's story. We never learn if he went inside. Why would Jesus leave that open? Who is supposed to finish the story?

Passage 3 — 2 Samuel 12:1-14

(Have someone read aloud.)

Questions:

7. Nathan confronts David with a parable. David is furious at the rich man who stole the poor man's lamb. Then Nathan says, "You are the man." David's response in verse 13 is immediate: "I have sinned against the LORD." And Nathan responds: "The LORD also has taken away your sin; you shall not die." The forgiveness is instant and complete. But read verses 10-14 carefully. What are the consequences that remain *after* the forgiveness? What does that tell you about the relationship between forgiveness and consequences?

8. "How could you?" — the question from Chapter 1 returns here. David was forgiven. Completely. Nathan said so on God's authority. But the sword never departed from his house. The child died. Psalm 51:3 says, "My sin is ever before me." David lived with forgiveness *and* consequences for the rest of his life. What does that mean for someone who has been forgiven by God and by their family, but who must still live with what their choices produced?

Passage 4 — 2 Corinthians 2:5-11

(Have someone read aloud.)

Questions:

9. Paul tells the church to forgive and comfort the repentant man, "so that he will not be overwhelmed by excessive sorrow" (v. 7). There is a real danger here — the danger of making the cost of return so high that the person is crushed by it. How do you welcome someone back without minimizing what happened, and without making restoration so punitive that it destroys them?

10. Verse 11 says "so that no advantage would be taken of us by Satan." What advantage does Satan gain when a repentant person is refused restoration? And what advantage does he gain when sin is treated as though it never happened?

The Two Tracks

Track A — For the One in the Struggle

A1. The father ran. He did not wait for the perfect speech. He saw the direction the son was walking and he ran. Are you walking in that direction? Not perfectly. Not with the right words. Just walking toward the Father. That is enough to start.

A2. David was forgiven — fully, immediately. And David lived with consequences for the rest of his life. "My sin is ever before me." If you have done things that created victims, that destroyed trust, that left damage behind — forgiveness does not erase those things. But forgiveness is real. Both things are true. Can you hold them both?

A3. The older brother represents everyone who will struggle with your return. Not everyone will celebrate. Some will resent it. Some will keep score. You cannot control that. What you can control is whether you keep walking toward the Father — regardless of who is angry about it.

Track B — For the Family

B1. The father ran. That was grace in action. But notice what the father *did not* do: he did not chase the son into the far country. He did not fund the rebellion. He did not pretend nothing happened. He waited, he watched, and when the son turned, he ran. Are you in a place where you can run when you see the turn? Or are you too hurt, too exhausted, too angry? Be honest. And bring that honesty to God.

B2. The older brother may be you. Not in his hostility, necessarily, but in his weariness. "I have been serving you all these years." You have been faithful. You have been present. You have carried the weight. And now the one who walked away gets the robe and the ring and the feast. If that feels unfair, you are not wrong to feel it. But read the father's response in verse 31. "All that is mine is yours." Your faithfulness was never unnoticed. Can you hear the Father say that to you?

B3. 2 Samuel 12:13 — David was forgiven. But the consequences remained. If your loved one has repented — genuinely — you may need to forgive. But trust is different from forgiveness. Forgiveness can be immediate. Trust must be earned. You are not failing if you forgive and still cannot fully trust yet. That is honest, and honesty is where healing begins.

Memory Verse

"But while he was still a long way off, his father saw him and felt compassion for him, and ran and embraced him and kissed him."

— Luke 15:20 (NASB)

For the Week Ahead

Read Luke 15:20-24 once this week. Then read 2 Samuel 12:13 — "The LORD also has taken away your sin." Sit with the tension between those two realities: grace that runs toward you, and consequences that remain behind you. Both are real. Both are true. Living with both is what the road looks like from here.

THE LONG ROAD

Chapter 9 — "The Long Road"

Before the Group Meets

Read Chapter 9 of *Change the Mind, Change the Man.*

Then read:

- **Galatians 6:1-5**
- **Philippians 3:12-16**
- **1 Corinthians 10:12-13**
- **Genesis 39:7-12**
- **Daniel 3:16-18**
- **2 Timothy 2:22**
- **1 Corinthians 15:33**
- **Matthew 12:43-45**

Opening

Have someone read Philippians 3:13-14 aloud.

> *"Brethren, I do not regard myself as having laid hold of it yet; but one thing I do: forgetting what lies behind and reaching forward to what lies ahead, I press on toward the goal for the prize of the upward call of God in Christ Jesus."*

Then ask: **What verb does Paul use to describe the Christian life?**

He says "I press on." Not "I have arrived." Not "I coasted." He *presses.* The word implies effort, strain, deliberate forward motion. And he says it after saying "I do not regard myself as having laid hold of it yet." The apostle Paul — the man who wrote half the New Testament — did not consider himself finished. The road is long. And the walking is daily.

Into the Text

Passage 1 — Galatians 6:1-5

(Have someone read aloud.)

Questions:

1. Verse 1: "Even if anyone is caught in any trespass, you who are spiritual, restore such a one in a spirit of gentleness." The word "restore" is the Greek *katartizō* — the same word used in Matthew 4:21 for mending fishing nets. It means to repair, to set right, to put back into working order. What does that image tell you about what restoration actually looks like? It is not pretending the net was never torn. It is mending it so it can function again.

2. The same verse adds: "each one looking to yourself, so that you too will not be tempted." The person doing the restoring is warned about their own vulnerability. Why? What does this prevent? And how does this apply to the family or the church member walking alongside someone in recovery?

3. Verse 2 says "bear one another's burdens." Verse 5 says "each one will bear his own load." Is that a contradiction? (Look more closely: "burden" in verse 2 is a word for a crushing weight — something too heavy for one person. "Load" in verse 5 is a soldier's pack — the daily responsibility each person carries.) How do you help someone carry what is crushing them without carrying what is theirs to carry?

Passage 2 — Philippians 3:12-16

(Have someone read aloud.)

Questions:

4. Paul says "I do not regard myself as having laid hold of it yet." He is not done. He is still pressing forward. If the apostle Paul could say that, what does it tell someone in recovery who feels like they should be further along? And what does it tell the family waiting for perfection?

5. "Forgetting what lies behind and reaching forward to what lies ahead." Paul does not say "pretend the past didn't happen." He says he does not let it define his direction. He is not looking backward while walking forward. What does the difference look like in daily practice?

6. Verse 16: "Let us keep living by that same standard to which we have attained." Paul says to hold the ground you have gained. Don't slide back. What does that look like practically — for the one in recovery, and for the family?

Passage 3 — 1 Corinthians 10:12-13

(Have someone read aloud.)

Questions:

7. Verse 12: "Therefore let him who thinks he stands take heed that he does not fall." The moment you think you are safe is often the moment before the fall. Why is that warning essential for recovery? What does overconfidence look like in this context?

8. Verse 13: "No temptation has overtaken you but such as is common to man; and God is faithful, who will not allow you to be tempted beyond what you are able, but with the temptation will provide the way of escape also, so that you will be able to endure it." God provides "the way of escape." Not the absence of temptation. The way *through* it. What does it mean to look for the escape rather than waiting for the temptation to disappear?

Passage 4 — Genesis 39:7-12, Daniel 3:16-18, and 2 Timothy 2:22

(Have someone read Genesis 39:7-12 aloud.)

Questions:

9. Joseph did not negotiate. He did not linger. He did not say "let me think about it." When Potiphar's wife grabbed him, verse 12 says "he left his garment in her hand and fled, and went outside." He left his coat behind — he did not even stop to collect his things. He *ran*. What does that tell you about how Joseph had already decided what he would do before the moment came? And what does it mean for someone in recovery that the decision to flee must be made *before* the temptation arrives?

10. Now read 2 Timothy 2:22: "Now flee from youthful lusts and pursue righteousness, faith, love and peace, with those who call on the Lord from a pure heart." Paul uses the word *flee* — the same kind of running Joseph did. He does not say "resist." He does not say "manage." He says *flee*. And notice what immediately follows the fleeing: "pursue righteousness, faith, love and peace, *with those who call on the Lord*." The fleeing and the pursuing happen together. You run *from* something and *to* something — and you do it with people. What does that look like practically for someone on the long road?

11. Now read Daniel 3:16-18. When King Nebuchadnezzar commanded everyone to bow down and worship the golden image, Shadrach, Meshach, and Abed-nego refused. The king gave them a second chance — and their answer was: "O Nebuchadnezzar, we do not need to give you an answer concerning this matter." They did not need time to think about it. The decision had already been made. They were not deciding in the moment whether to bow. They had already decided they would not. Joseph ran because his mind was already made up. These three men stood because their minds were already made up. What do these two examples — one about fleeing, one about standing — tell you about when the real decision happens? It does not happen in the moment of pressure. It happens before. Have you made that decision?

Passage 5 — 1 Corinthians 15:33

"Do not be deceived: 'Bad company corrupts good morals.'"

Questions:

12. This is a one-verse warning, and it is absolute. The company you keep will shape the person you become. The associations that changed during the descent (Week 2) must change again during the return — and stay changed. Why is this one of the hardest practical realities of recovery? And what does "do not be deceived" suggest about the temptation to think it won't matter?

Passage 6 — Matthew 12:43-45

(Have someone read aloud.)

Questions:

13. The unclean spirit leaves, finds the house "swept and put in order" — but empty — and returns with seven others worse. The house was cleaned out but not filled with anything new. What does this parable say about recovery that removes the substance but does not replace it with something? And what is the "something" that must fill the space?

The Two Tracks

Track A — For the One in the Struggle

A1. Philippians 3:13-14 — Paul presses on. The road is daily. Not daily inspiration. Daily discipline. What does your daily discipline look like right now? Bible study? Prayer? Being around the right people? If those things are missing, what fills the time instead?

A2. 1 Corinthians 10:12 — "let him who thinks he stands take heed that he does not fall." Have you had a moment of confidence — "I've got this" — that preceded a fall? What would humility look like in your daily walk?

A3. Joseph ran. He did not explain himself. He did not try to reason his way out. He left his coat in her hand and got out of the house. Have you decided — in advance, before the moment comes — what you will do when you find yourself somewhere you should not be? Not "I'll try to say no." That is not what Joseph did. He ran. What does your escape plan look like? And do you have one, or are you still assuming you will figure it out in the moment?

A4. 1 Corinthians 15:33 — "bad company corrupts good morals." Have you changed the people you spend time with? If not, why not? Be honest. Is it because you think you are strong enough, or because the old company is comfortable?

A5. Matthew 12:43-45 — the empty house. Your mind has been emptied of one thing. What are you filling it with? If the answer is "nothing," the passage warns you about what comes next. Philippians 4:8 gave you the list last week. Are you using it?

Track B — For the Family

B1. Galatians 6:2 says to bear one another's burdens. Verse 5 says each one will bear his own load. You cannot carry what belongs to them. But you can help carry what is crushing them — and what is crushing you. Who is helping you carry your burden right now? If the answer is "no one," that needs to change. James 5:16 said so two weeks ago.

B2. Trust is rebuilt in inches, not miles. The difference between forgiveness and trust is the difference between a decision and a process. Forgiveness can happen in a moment. Trust takes time, consistency, and kept promises. You are not failing your loved one by requiring evidence of change over time. You are being honest. And honesty is the only foundation trust can be built on.

B3. Philippians 3:16 — "keep living by that same standard to which we have attained." You have gained ground too — over these nine weeks, or over months and years of this journey. Don't give that ground back. What ground have you gained? And what threatens to take it from you?

Memory Verse

"Brethren, I do not regard myself as having laid hold of it yet; but one thing I do: forgetting what lies behind and reaching forward to what lies ahead, I press on toward the goal for the prize of the upward call of God in Christ Jesus. "

— Philippians 3:13-14 (NASB)

For the Week Ahead

Read 1 Corinthians 10:12-13 each day this week. And read Genesis 39:12 once — just the one verse. Joseph left his garment and fled. He did not hesitate. He did not negotiate. He ran. When the temptation comes — and it will, in whatever form it takes for you — look for the way of escape. God promised it would be there. Your job is not to eliminate the temptation. Your job is to take the exit when God provides it, the way Joseph did. Don't walk. Run. And He will provide it.

THE GOD WHO FINDS YOU

Chapter 10 — "The God Who Finds You"

Before the Group Meets

Read Chapter 10 of *Change the Mind, Change the Man.*

Then read:

- **Acts 2:36-41**
- **Romans 6:1-7**
- **Acts 22:6-16**
- **Romans 10:9-10, 13-17**

Opening

Have someone read Acts 22:16 aloud.

> *"Now why do you delay? Get up and be baptized, and wash away your sins, calling on His name."*

Then ask: **What question does Ananias ask Saul — and what is the only honest answer?**

"Why do you delay?" There is no good answer to that question. Saul — later Paul the apostle — had seen the Lord on the Damascus road. He had been blind for three days. He had been praying. And Ananias did not say "think about it" or "when you're ready." He said, "Why do you delay? Get up." The urgency is not manufactured. It is the natural response to the truth. If this is true — if Jesus is Lord, if sins need washing, if God is offering what the entire book has been pointing toward — then delay is the only thing that doesn't make sense.

Into the Text

Passage 1 — Romans 10:9-10, 13-17

(Have someone read aloud.)

Questions:

1. Verse 9: "If you confess with your mouth Jesus as Lord, and believe in your heart that God raised Him from the dead, you will be saved." Paul identifies two things: confession with the mouth, belief in the heart. Why both? Why is internal belief not enough by itself? And why is outward confession not enough without internal belief?

2. Verse 17: "So faith comes from hearing, and hearing by the word of Christ." Where does faith begin? Not in a feeling. Not in a personal experience. Faith comes from *hearing the word*. You have been hearing the word for ten weeks. What has it produced in you?

Passage 2 — Acts 2:36-41

(Have someone read aloud.)

Questions:

3. Verse 37: "They were pierced to the heart, and said to Peter and the rest of the apostles, 'Brethren, what shall we do?'" The crowd heard the truth about Jesus, and it pierced them. They did not ask "what should we think about?" They asked "what shall we *do?*" What does Peter tell them to do in verse 38?

4. Verse 38: "Repent, and each of you be baptized in the name of Jesus Christ for the forgiveness of your sins." Peter does not separate repentance from baptism. He does not offer one without the other. What is the stated purpose — "for the forgiveness of your sins." If this book has been about the mind turning back to God, this is where the turning becomes concrete and complete. What does repentance mean in this verse? (Remember Week 7 — Luke 15:17-20. The prodigal did not just think about going home. He got up and went.)

5. Verse 41: "Those who had received his word were baptized; and that day there were added about three thousand souls." They received the word. They were baptized. They were added. This is the New Testament pattern — not one element, but the complete response. How many of these three thousand do you think had their whole life figured out first? And what does that tell you about who this invitation is for?

Passage 3 — Romans 6:1-7

(Have someone read aloud.)

Questions:

6. Verses 3-4: "Do you not know that all of us who have been baptized into Christ Jesus have been baptized into His death? Therefore we have been buried with Him through baptism into death, so that as Christ was raised from the dead through the glory of the Father, so we too might walk in newness of life." Paul says baptism is a burial and a resurrection. The old person is buried. A new person is raised. What does that imagery mean for someone coming out of addiction? What is being buried? And what is being raised?

7. Verse 6: "Knowing this, that our old self was crucified with Him, in order that our body of sin might be done away with, so that we would no longer be slaves to sin." The old self is crucified. The slavery is broken. In Week 4, John 8:34 said "everyone who commits sin is the slave of sin." And John 8:36 said "if the Son makes you free, you will be free indeed." Romans 6 tells you how that freedom happens. What is the connection between what Jesus did and what happens in baptism?

Passage 4 — Acts 22:6-16

(Have someone read aloud.)

Questions:

8. Saul — the man who persecuted Christians, who approved of Stephen's death, who was on his way to arrest believers in Damascus — was stopped by the Lord Himself. If God could reach Saul on that road, is there anyone beyond His reach?

9. Ananias said "why do you delay?" Saul had every reason to feel unworthy. He had blood on his hands. He had spent years fighting against the very truth he now believed. And Ananias did not tell him to go prove himself first. He told him to get up. What does that say to the person who believes they have done too much, gone too far, or waited too long?

The Two Tracks

Track A — For the One in the Struggle

A1. You have spent ten weeks in Scripture. You have heard the truth about the mind turning from God and the mind turning back. You have read about grace that runs, about forgiveness that is real and complete, about a new creation. The question is the same question Ananias asked Saul: *Why do you delay?*

If you have not obeyed the gospel — if you have not believed, repented, confessed Jesus as Lord, and been baptized for the forgiveness of your sins — then everything this book has described is waiting for you. Not when you are cleaned up. Not when you are worthy. Now.

If you have obeyed the gospel before and walked away, the Father is on the road. He has been watching. He sees you. And He will run.

A2. Romans 6:4 — "walk in newness of life." That is what the long road looks like with God in it. Not perfection. Newness. The old person buried, the new person raised. Are you ready to bury the old?

Track B — For the Family

B1. This chapter is not only for the addict. It is for anyone who reaches this point and realizes they need the foundation this book has been describing. You may have been going through this crisis — this entire journey — without being grounded in Christ yourself. Or you may have wandered from the foundation you once had. The invitation is for you too.

B2. Acts 22:16 — "Why do you delay?" That question may apply to your loved one. But it may also apply to you. What have you been delaying? Not just regarding the gospel, but regarding your own walk with God, your own spiritual health, your own need for renewal? James 4:14 — you are a vapor too. Don't put off what matters most while waiting for someone else's crisis to resolve.

B3. If your loved one has come to faith, or returned to faith, through this study — remember the father. He ran. The robe, the ring, the feast. Full restoration. Not trust rebuilt in a day — that takes time. But love without hesitation. That is what the Father models. Can you follow His example?

Memory Verse

"Now why do you delay? Get up and be baptized, and wash away your sins, calling on His name."

— Acts 22:16 (NASB)

For the Week Ahead — and Beyond

This study is finished. The book is finished. But the road is not.

If you obeyed the gospel during this study, the walk begins now — and it is the walk described in Week 9: daily, deliberate, sustained. Get into the word every day. Be with God's people. Set your mind on things above. Press on.

If you have been walking the road for a while, keep walking. Philippians 3:14 — press on toward the goal.

If you led this group, thank you. What you did — sitting with people in the text week after week — is what faithful Bible teaching looks like. You can lead this study again with another group. The text does not expire. The need does not diminish. And you now know the way.

The book began with a phone call. It ends with a Father who runs. Between those two moments is the entire human story — the turning away and the turning back. The substance was never the real problem. The gaze was. Fix it on Christ. Keep it there. And walk.

Study guide for use with Change the Mind, Change the Man *by Paul Hainline. Scripture quotations from the New American Standard Bible® (NASB). Copyright © The Lockman Foundation. Used by permission.*